TRAINING TO SUCCEED

Judo

Rita Storey

W
FRANKLIN WATTS
LONDON•SYDNEY

First published in 2010 by
Franklin Watts
338 Euston Road
London NW1 3BH

Franklin Watts Australia
Level 17/207 Kent Street
Sydney NSW 2000

Words in **bold** are in the glossary on page 30.

Series editor: Julia Bird
Art director: Jonathan Hair

Series designed and created for Franklin Watts by Storeybooks.
Designer: Rita Storey
Editor: Nicola Barber
Photography: Tudor Photography, Banbury (unless otherwise stated)

Picture credits

All photographs Tudor Photography, Banbury unless otherwise stated.
Julian Finney/Getty Images p27, FRANCK FIFE/AFP/Getty Images p26.

Thanks to Luke Preston of the Camberley Judo Club,
(www.camberleyjudo.co.uk) for all his help. Also thanks to Josh Butler,
Nathon Burns, Robyn Irwin and Sam Hughes for their participation in
the book.

A CIP catalogue record for this book is available from the
British Library.

Dewey classification: 796.8'152
ISBN: 978 0 7496 9541 5

Printed in China

Franklin Watts is a division of Hachette
Children's Books, an Hachette UK company.
www.hachette.co.uk

Contents

Meet the judoka

Judo is a **Japanese** martial art **that is also a fast and exciting Olympic sport. Martial arts are fighting sports. The object of judo is to unbalance your opponent so that you can throw him or her to the ground. You then try to hold your opponent down for a period of time, or until he or she** submits. **Points are scored for the technique of the throws and hold-downs, and for an opponent's submission. Someone who takes part in judo is called a** judoka.

*Judo, which means 'the gentle way', was developed from **jujitsu**, an ancient Japanese fighting art. In 1882 a Japanese jujitsu expert called Jigoro Kano made changes to jujitsu to make it safe as a competitive sport. This new sport became known as judo.*

In this book you will meet four judoka who are part of the **elite** training programme at Camberley Judo Club. You can read about their experiences of what it is like to train to compete at the highest level.

Nathon Burns

I am 20 years old. I compete in the Under 60kg weight, the lightest men's weight division in senior judo. I have been training full time for four years now. I left school at 16 and moved to a training centre in Walsall, and from there to Camberley. With the amount of judo training I do, I don't get much of a chance to have any other hobbies.

Coach's comment

Nathon Burns is one of the most exciting and technical judoka in the Under 23 (U23) age group. In 2008 he competed at the Junior European and World championships. He has already made his mark at senior **tournaments** with two medals at the Swiss Open and British Open.

Josh Butler

I am 17 years old. I compete in the 90kg weight. I'm training full time and live at the club. As well as judo, I enjoy reading and listening to music.

Coach's comment

Josh Butler has only been doing judo for three years, but since he began full-time training he has accelerated on to the junior national team. He is currently ranked number two in his division in the junior age group.

Robyn Irwin

I am 15 years old. I compete in the Under 63kg weight.

I train half time, which is three sessions a day, two-and-a-half days a week. When I am training I also live at the club. As well as judo, I enjoy photography, fashion and interior design, writing – and more judo!

Coach's comment

Robyn Irwin is one of our most dedicated juniors at the club. She is the youngest and most inexperienced in our elite training group, but with her desire to succeed she is improving all the time.

Sam Hughes

I am 17 years old. I compete in the Under 55kg weight. I train five days a week but I live at home. As well as judo, I enjoy socialising with friends.

Coach's comment

Sam Hughes has recently begun full-time training. Already a **cadet** national and international champion (see page 6), the move up to a new age group means he must put on weight. He has taken to this challenge wholeheartedly with supplementary weight training and **nutrition**.

Judo in the Olympics

Judo has been an Olympic sport for men since 1964. Women have only been allowed to compete for judo medals at the Olympic Games since 1992. Japan has the most judo medals. Great Britain has not yet won a gold medal for judo.

If they train hard, maybe Nathon, Robyn, Josh or Sam will win an Olympic gold medal.

Starting out

Young people choose to take up a particular sport for a range of different reasons – maybe because there is a good club nearby, or maybe because family members are already involved in the sport.

Local clubs

Most young people start judo as a fun activity at their local club. In the early stages, boys and girls train together.

Between the ages of eight and 15, there are 18 grades, known as **Mon** (junior) grades. There is a different colour belt (**obi**) for every fourth Mon.

From age 16 there are **Kyu** (senior) grades. These also have different coloured belts. Once players have worked their way up through all the grades, they become 1st **Dan** grade and wear a black belt. Even in the Dan grade there are ten more levels to achieve.

Developing talent

The England Talent Development Programme has been set up to encourage and develop the best English judoka.

Elite training
Some judo clubs offer high-level training for those on the England Talent Development Programme.

British U20 Championships
Judoka who qualify through area trials can enter the British Championships. Medallists from some age categories are selected for their country's cadet squads (England, Scotland, Wales and Northern Ireland). They may also be chosen to fight for the Great Britain cadet team in international championships.

British Senior Championships
The medallists from this event form the GB senior squad.

Coach's notes: competitions

Whatever your grade, there will be an opportunity to compete with other judoka at a similar level in your club. There are mini-Mon competitions for beginners, pre-cadet, cadet and junior competitions. All competitions have age, weight and grade restrictions to ensure that players of similar abilities are paired together in contests.

I started doing judo when I was 13. My dad is a black belt and has been involved with judo since he was at school. He thought taking up judo would be a good way of keeping me out of trouble!

Starting judo so late meant I had a lot of catching up to do. I used to get beaten all the time.

I was five when my dad first introduced me to judo. I was a very active kid and loved to watch the Power Rangers *and Bruce Lee. I begged and begged my parents to let me do something similar.*

Most of my family are or have been involved in judo at some stage. My dad (Joe Burns) is a successful coach back in my home town. My brothers all do judo. My eldest brother, Joseph Burns, trained full time and represented Great Britain at the cadet Europeans, and my two younger brothers do judo with my dad. One of my sisters also did judo when she was younger, but gave it up to concentrate on dancing.

I started doing judo when I was six. My dad got me into it. My first club was Fleet and Frogmore Judo Club.

My family and my first coach, Bernie Earle at Camberley Judo Club, all encouraged me when I first started to compete.

I started doing judo when I was eight years old because I wanted to learn self-defence. My first club was in Portsmouth. I also used to do athletics and fencing, but I always enjoyed judo and worked hardest at it.

My mum and dad have always encouraged me. They made sure that fighting was fun – win or lose.

Judo is a physically demanding sport. It is also very disciplined.

7

The coach

Good coaching is a vital part of a judo player's career. A coach is responsible not only for the physical development and training of the judoka in his care, but also for motivating and supporting them.

The role of a coach

It is the coach's job to develop an individual training programme and assess a player's needs in both the short and long term. Luke Preston is the senior coach at Camberley Judo Club and runs the full-time elite programme there. He meets with each player every week to agree a schedule of training.

Individual needs

Judoka on the elite training programme are a mixture of ages and abilities. Some need to fit in part-time jobs to fund their training, others are still working for exams and have homework to do. For those who are living at the club, it may be their first time away from home, and they may need help adjusting.

Meet the coach: Luke Preston

Since 2005, when I retired from competition, I have been a full-time judo coach. I was a Wales and GB international for many years and won bronze at the Manchester Commonwealth Games. As well as coaching at the club, I also work as a support coach for the British team at Junior (U20) and U23 levels. This has seen me coach at the Junior European, Junior World and European U23 championships.

Luke is good at motivating me – he pushes me harder than I would push myself. The fact that he believes in me really helps in competitions. He also watches for mistakes and tells me how to iron them out.

Luke sits down with Robyn to discuss her individual weekly training schedule.

Luke and Sam watch a video of a recent competition to assess how well Sam performed.

Weekly programme

The weekly programme agreed between the coach and player covers all aspects of training and development. For example, because Sam has recently moved up to a new age group, he needs to put on some weight. He and Luke carefully monitor his nutrition and weight training to see how he is progressing.

Setting goals

Coaches use a variety of different methods to get the best out of their players. Setting achievable goals is one way of encouraging better performance. Using video playback of competitions is also a useful way to analyse strengths and weaknesses. Luke shows his players videos of matches so that they can see where things went wrong (or right).

Luke is a great coach and an awesome friend. The effort and passion he puts into all of us is unbelievable. He helps us not just on the mat and with training, but with our lives in general.

The training programme he sets out for us is very clever. Sometimes we don't realise the thought behind the programme – but we trust him and that's why we keep on improving.

Luke is very composed, patient and supportive. He helps with technique and weight training and does all he can to make competitions go smoothly.

When my attitude is right he gives me supportive feedback – if my attitude isn't right, he will tell me.

Training

Judo is an extremely demanding sport. Competitors have to be physically strong and very flexible. They need a high level of general fitness, as well as the ability to find a burst of explosive energy when necessary.

A typical day's training

A typical day of training for Robyn, Sam, Josh and Nathon starts at 10.00 a.m. with their first judo session. In this session they practise the technical aspects of judo. This lasts for one-and-a-half hours and is followed by a 30-minute break to rest and refuel. Then there is strength and **conditioning** training from 12.00 to 1.30 p.m. In the afternoon there is time for more food, rest and study. In the evening the judoka return to the training room (**dojo**) for **Randori** (sparring practice, see pages 18–19) between 8.00 and 9.30 p.m.

Warming up

The judoka start each training session by warming up with a game of touch rugby. This type of activity is called **cardiovascular exercise**. It is designed to increase the heart rate and strengthen the heart and lungs.

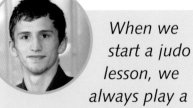

When we start a judo lesson, we always play a rugby game. This is fun and it warms our bodies and loosens us up. After that we go into Uchikomi *and different kinds of* Nage Komi *(throwing practice, see page 13). We have different warm ups and cool downs depending on what activity we're doing.*

Training sessions start with a warm-up game of touch rugby.

Sam stretches his muscles before a training session.

Robyn and Sam work on an Uchikomi exercise.

Preparing the muscles

The next part of the warm up is a series of stretches and **drills**. These exercises are designed to prepare all the muscles to work at their maximum. Doing this helps to prevent strains and muscle damage in the actual training session.

Second nature

There is no time in a contest to think about technique so it must be second nature to react in the right way. *Uchikomi* is a series of drills designed to build that automatic reaction. In *Uchikomi* the judoka practise the moves up to the point of an actual throw, but they do not follow it through. The drills are done rhythmically to music a set number of times before the judoka change places and begin again.

Grips and throws

Judo uses the least amount of physical strength necessary to throw an opponent. In order to do this, the judoka's technique and timing must be perfect.

Grip

You can win or lose a match by getting a good grip of your opponent, and by stopping your opponent getting a good grip on you. The art of taking a firm grip is called *Kumi Kata*. In judo you take hold of your opponent by gripping his or her jacket. There are various grips suitable for different pulling and hanging actions, and for the throw you intend to do.

Breaking balance

Once you have a good hold of your opponent the next stage is to force him or her off balance and execute a throw. Breaking your opponent's balance is called *Kuzushi*.

Types of throw

When you have your opponent off balance there are many different types of throw that you can use. Throwing technique is called *Nage Waza*. These are just a few of the different types:

Shoulder throws

Shoulder throws are the most spectacular to watch, but the most difficult to surprise your opponent with. They start with the attacker turning his or her back to an opponent and bending the knees. The power produced from straightening the legs forces the opponent off the floor and over the attacker's shoulder.

Uchi Mata (see page 13) is my favourite throw. If you get it right it's pretty hard for your opponent to stop even if he or she knows it's coming – but it's a very hard technique to master.

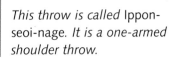

This throw is called Ippon-seoi-nage. *It is a one-armed shoulder throw.*

Uchi Mata *is an inner thigh throw. It is one of the most successful throws in competition.*

Everyone has favourite moves and throws. I love Uchi Mata. *I'm still trying to get better at it and* Tai Otoshi *(body drop). They are very nice throws to do.*

This throw, called Ouchi Gari, *is an example of a reaping throw.*

Hip throws

In a hip throw the attacker turns sideways to the opponent with bent knees. He or she then pulls the opponent over the hip and into the throw.

Reaping throws

In a **reaping** throw, the judoka uses his or her feet and legs to sweep an opponent's legs from under them.

Throwing practice

Repetitive practice throwing in a training session is called *Nage Komi*. It is a way of getting used to throwing and landing properly. It is often done after *Uchikomi* in a practice session (see page 11).

My favourite moves are Ouchi Gari *(large inner reaping throw) and* Osoto Gari *(large outer reaping throw).*

Groundwork

Throws are only one part of a judo contest. Unless you throw your opponent perfectly (*Ippon*) **and win the contest outright, the rest of the fight may take place down on the** tatami **(judo mat). Any moves done on the tatami are called** groundwork (*Ne Waza*)**.**

In groundwork the ways to win a competition are by **hold-downs** (*Osaekomi Waza*) and submission.

Hold-downs

A competition can be won by holding your opponent down for between 15 and 25 seconds (see page 24 for competition scoring). The judge will start timing a hold-down when the attacker is in the correct position – holding the defender on his or her back so that one or both shoulders are on the mat and the legs are free to move.

If during a hold-down the defender can lift his or her hips and back off the mat, the counting of the hold-down stops. This move is called **bridging**.

This is an example of a hold-down. It is called Kesa Gatame.

14

This armlock is called Juji Gatame.

A defender can also escape a hold-down by grabbing the opponent's leg with his or her legs. The referee will call *Toketa* (hold is broken).

Armlocks and strangles

Attacking techniques, such as armlocks that put pressure on the arm joints (*Kansetsu Waza*) and strangles that put pressure on the neck (*Shime Waza*), are done on the ground. These holds can be dangerous and the person in hold can submit at any time by tapping the mat twice. The attacker must then release the hold immediately. Respecting these rules means that armlocks and strangles can be attempted in training and competition with very little injury.

Coach's notes: being competitive

Being competitive is good, but being too competitive can be a hindrance. Too much focus on what others are doing and achieving does not help personal development. Competition within a training group should be fun, natural and healthy.

Strength and conditioning

You are more likely to win a judo contest if you are stronger and fitter than your opponent. Winning also requires ability, perfect timing and the right mental attitude, but if you are not physically fit you will not get the opportunity to put these skills into practice.

Types of exercise

For Nathon, Robyn, Josh and Sam the middle session each day is dedicated to strength and conditioning training. These exercises are part of each student's weekly training programme and are different for every individual. Sam is trying to build muscle and put on weight, so he is working with weights. Nathon needs to keep his weight steady to compete in the Under 60kg group. His programme includes running, especially in the lead-up to a competition.

Josh lifts weights to increase his upper body strength.

These pull-ups (top) help Sam to increase his upper body strength and to build muscle. Tying a weight to his back (bottom) makes the exercise even harder.

Moving to a heavier weight group has been hard. I still weigh less than 50kg, so in the Under 55kg group I am usually fighting people heavier than me.

Nathon helps
Robyn to train.
She is throwing a
heavy medicine
ball as she does
sit-ups. This exercise
helps to improve her
core strength (see below).

Core strength

In all physically demanding sports, athletes train to improve their core strength – the strength of the muscles in the main part of the body. Good core strength helps to prevent injuries.

Stamina

Stamina is the ability to perform at a high level for long periods. Tiredness towards the end of a competition can cause a loss of performance. Running and other **aerobic exercises** help to build stamina.

When athletes push themselves hard, a substance called **lactic acid** builds up in their muscles and causes pain. High-intensity **circuit training** gets their muscles used to this build-up, and so reduces the pain.

Cooling down

At the end of a training session, the judoka do a series of stretches to stop their muscles stiffening up and **cramping**.

Nathon runs to increase his stamina and keep his weight down.

I hated running until I came to Camberley. But with the woods and the views around here you can't help but enjoy it.

Randori

Randori is sparring practice. It is an opportunity to put all the skills used in Uchikomi and Nage Komi (see pages 11 and 13) into practice.

For Robyn, Nathan, Sam and Josh, *Randori* is the third and most physically demanding training session of the day. The judoka are paired up and are able to use the techniques they have been practising against a resisting opponent.

A good *Randori* session is as close as the judoka will get to a competition situation. There are no set patterns of moves to follow, so the judoka must use their skills and timing to find a good grip. They must also choose the right move to beat their partners, while maintaining a strong defence. Without the pressure of having to win, the judoka can try out moves that they are still unsure of, as well as perfecting those that they know well.

Luke watches a group of judoka doing Ne Waza (groundwork) Randori. *Upright* Randori *is called* Tachi Waza.

Sam Lowe (left), a member of the Camberley elite squad, trains with Danny Lowe in Randori practice.

Defending

As well as practising throws and holds, the judoka have an opportunity in *Randori* to perfect their defensive moves. In a judo contest, a competitor must be able to avoid being thrown without being too defensive. If a competitor does not attack enough, points can be awarded to his or her opponent.

Different partners

In competitions judoka are grouped by age and weight. In a *Randori* session, judoka often face a wide range of different opponents. The art of judo is to use the force of an attack against an attacker. This means that, if he or she has good technique, a smaller or younger judoka can be a match for a bigger or older opponent.

I love Randori – fighting is the best bit. I don't like running (especially in the rain).

Improvement

Randori is also an opportunity for a coach to watch the judoka in action. The coach will be making mental notes of what moves they need to work on, and what adjustments to make to an individual's training schedule.

Safety and respect

Jujitsu, the Japanese martial art from which judo developed, was practised by Buddhist monks as a way of defending themselves.

Reducing the risk

Judo is a potentially dangerous sport. It is also a sport that puts a lot of emphasis on self-control and discipline. Judoka learn to respect themselves and to respect others. Thanks to this strict code of discipline, judo can be practised without too much risk of injury.

Learning to fall

The first thing a judoka learns is how to fall safely. Techniques of falling safely are called *Ukemi*, or **breakfalls**. The idea of a breakfall is to spread your weight as you hit the mat. It is important to protect your head, spine and neck when you fall. Judoka do this by tucking their head in and striking the mat hard with one or both arms. There are different types of breakfall, depending on which way you land.

Other safety points to remember
- Never leave anything on the judo mat.
- Move tables and chairs well away from the mat area.
- Always train with a qualified judo instructor.
- Have someone available who is qualified in first aid.
- Do not wear any jewellery.

Tapping out

A judoka can submit at any time by tapping the mat twice. Once in a hold that is putting pressure on a joint, it is vital that the defender taps out as soon as they realise they cannot escape. The attacker must let go as soon as they are aware of a submission.

Robyn practises a back breakfall.

I was in the semi-finals of the English Open. My opponent tried to block my arm and trapped it. He put pressure on it and I pulled my arm out. After that I couldn't lift my arm. I tried to carry on, but eventually I had to drop out.

I went for an X-ray and I had snapped a piece of bone in my elbow. The surgeon fixed it all up. I had the operation 12 weeks ago and I started **physio** *a couple of days after the operation. I was back on the mat seven to eight weeks later, which is very shocking to a lot of people. My arm is still tender and still on the mend – but I'm back to fighting!*

Not tapping out early enough, or not letting go quickly enough, can both lead to injury.

Respect

When Jigoro Kano developed judo, his basic principle was 'mutual benefit and prosperity'. He believed that one person should not progress at the expense of others. His instructors and students were expected to uphold the values of honesty and good behaviour.

Judo is still a sport that believes in respect and self-discipline. Judoka still bow (*Rei wo suru*) to each other at the beginning and end of every competition and practice session.

Judoka bow to each other before a training session. The bow is a sign of respect, and part of judo's strict code of discipline.

Lifestyle

Learning to balance judo training with work and a social life can be very difficult. There are sacrifices that have to be made, but these judoka think it is all worth it.

I fit in a part-time job in the afternoons between lunch and my evening training session. Having a job is good because it helps to fund my judo training.

Academic work

Many judo academies give young players the opportunity to live in, so that they do not have to travel to and from training sessions. The Camberley Judo Club has full-time, day and half-time academy students.

Organisation

Joining a judo academy may mean living away from home for the first time. Learning to look after themselves is a new challenge for most young judoka. They have to make sure that they eat the right diet and keep themselves fit and healthy.

One thing about living away from home that Josh does not enjoy is having to cook his own meals!

Josh and Nathon live at the judo club. Robyn is there half-time and Sam travels in for training every day.

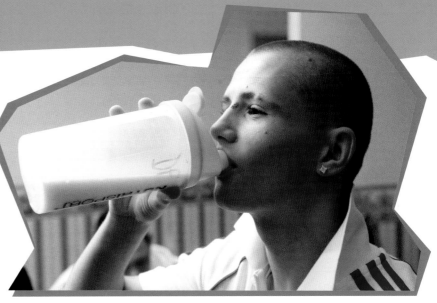

Sam lives at home so he does not have to worry about cooking for himself. He drinks protein shakes to increase his weight.

Social life

Dedicating yourself to a sport at a young age can mean missing out on leisure time and seeing friends. Most young judoka feel that achieving their goals makes up for the sacrifices they have to make.

Living with a group of people who are dedicated to judo can be a very good thing. Strong friendships are made through a shared love of the sport.

Robyn is considering training to be an architect at some time in the future. She needs to keep up with her studies.

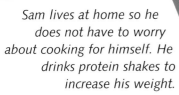

I'm home schooled and doing my GCSEs when I'm not training. This means I don't get time off at weekends, as I work through them unless I'm competing. I miss my younger brother and sister, and they are always complaining they don't see me enough.

I love what I'm doing and where I am. It's all worth it because I'm enjoying the journey.

Competitions

As you progress in any sport, it is natural to want to test yourself against the abilities of others of your own age, weight and skill. Judo tournaments are organised at local club, national and international levels.

Weighing in

To enter a tournament, you need to register and be weighed to see what weight group you will fight in.

Before a fight begins, one out of every pair of opponents is either given a blue belt to wear in addition to his or her own obi (belt), or asked to wear a blue **judogi** (judo uniform).

There are three referees in a contest. Two sit at opposite corners of the mat, and the third moves around the mat. The referee on the mat signals the results. The decisions of the referees are final.

On the day of a competition, I drink lots and eat energy food. Long car journeys or nerves can be draining.

I'm very anti-social before a fight. I'd never talk to anyone except my coach – it would only distract me. Listening to music helps.

If there's space by the mat I pace up and down. I don't really think about anything, just about walking on the mat. I like to know if my opponent is left- or right-handed – I'm more relaxed if I know that.

Scoring in a judo competition

In a judo competition points are scored for the quality of the throws and hold-downs.

Yuko – 5 points
A throw in which the thrown player lands on one side of his or her back.
A 20-second hold-down.

Wazari – 7 points
A throw in which the thrown player lands almost flat on his or her back.
A 25-second hold-down.

Ippon – 10 points
A continuous, clean throw in which the thrown player's shoulders and back touch the mat at the same time.
A 30-second hold-down.
Submission – from an armlock, strangle or retirement from injury.

An *Ippon* score wins a contest outright. Two *Wazari* scores from a player make *Wazari-aweseti-ippon* – a 10-point score.

If an *Ippon* has not been scored by the end of the time limit, the player with the highest score wins.

Time limits: Senior – 5 minutes
Junior – 4 minutes

Listening to music is a good way to block out distractions before a competition.

Before a competition, I have to do a lot more fat-burning sessions to lose weight for my weight category. I still need to have enough energy though – so I put in different runs and exercises in between sessions.

Types of contest

There are different ways of organising judo competitions. All are based on a series of knock-out contests in which the winner of each fight moves on to fight another opponent.

Major judo competitions work on a system called **repechage**. The contestants are split into two groups, or tables. Within each table the winner of a match goes on to fight again until only four contestants remain in each table. The four losing quarter-finalists become the repechage group. The two winners of the repechage group fight the two losing semi-finalists for the bronze medal.

Contestants who lost to the finalists in each table fight again, and the winners of each loser group fight the loser of the main final for second or third place.

Golden score rule

In the 2004 Olympics a new rule was added. If the score is level at the end of the time limit (see page 24), the scoreboard is cleared. Golden score time (three minutes for seniors, two minutes for juniors) then starts. The first score (or penalty) after the clock is restarted for golden score time wins.

Coach's notes: preparation

Before stepping on to the mat to compete in a key event, the judoka must know that they have done all they can to perform at their optimum. They must be prepared mentally as well as physically, and be able to visualise themselves winning. No stone must be left unturned!

Sporting heroes

Top-level judoka are an inspiration to those who want to follow in their footsteps. But judoka do not have to be Olympic medallists to inspire others. Judoka from local clubs who show real dedication to their sport can be a great influence on younger players as well.

Japan's Takamasa Anai (in white) battles with France's Pierre Robin in the 2008 World Judo Championships in Paris, France.

My judo hero is John Buchanan. He was a lightweight fighter who started at Camberley Judo Club at a young age. He is an ex-coach of mine, and a good friend.

I really enjoy watching the Japanese heavyweights fight. Their technique and speed is awesome to watch. My favourite at the moment is Takamasa Anai.

Self-defence

Many young people take judo classes today to learn self-defence skills, as well as to exercise. The strict codes of practice and levels of self-control taught in judo mean that not only do judoka stay fit and safe – they can also become positive role models for other young people.

Craig Fallon, the British Under 60kg World Champion in 2005, is my judo hero.

Craig is one of my good friends and I used to train with him a few years ago. He's not only a very talented judo player, he is also very humble – a really nice guy.

I hope to be able to accomplish some of the things he has done in his judo career. I think it's good that he has done the things he has but still remained the same person.

Craig Fallon
Great Britain
Weight: 60kg
Date of birth: 18 Dec 1982

Olympian in 2008 Olympic Games in Beijing
2007 Men's World Cup
2006 European Championships: Gold
2005 World Championships: Gold
2004 Prague 'A' Tournament: Gold
2003 World Championships: Silver
2003 Rome 'A' Tournament: Gold
2003 Paris Super 'A' Tournament: Gold
2003 European Championships: Silver
2002 Commonwealth Games: Gold

Craig Fallon (in blue) of Great Britain takes on Kim Kyong-Jin of North Korea during the men's Under 60kg repechage at the 2008 Olympic Games in Beijing, China.

The next step

Dedication, skill, talent and an element of good luck are all vital for judo players to make it to the top of their sport.

Some judoka continue to compete at the highest level into their late twenties or early thirties, but judo is a physical sport and injuries do happen. Players often continue in the sport as coaches after their playing career is over, passing on their expertise to a new generation of competitors.

International competitions

For sportsmen and women there is something very special about representing their country at international level. In judo there are European and World championships at both junior and senior levels, open to male and female judoka.

Eyes on the prize

The ultimate prize for the judoka featured in this book is to win a gold medal at the Olympic Games, which are held every four years. The four judoka are all at different stages on the ladder towards that goal. It will take a lot of hard work, and there will be lows as well as highs on the way, but they are all training hard to succeed.

Coach's notes: what it takes to succeed

Lots of talented judo players have not had the dedication to reach the top. Maybe dedication and the will to succeed are really what we define as talent.

Great Britain seriously needs to win a gold at Olympic judo. In five years' time I would like to be British number one and an Olympian. First I need to train like an animal and win medals in the Junior World and European championships.

My ambition is to do well in the World Championships and the Olympics.

I would like to join the Royal Navy and have a career in judo as well. I want to be the best I possibly can.

My ambition is to represent my country in London 2012 and win an Olympic medal.

I have many small goals on the way to that ambition, including winning medals in the 'A' tournaments, which are the next level below Olympics and World Championships.

Judo has been changing a lot recently. Japan and some of the other Asian countries used to dominate the sport, but there are now a lot of other countries coming through. From watching the last Olympics and World Championships, it's clear that if you have the right training, determination and mindset you can win.

If I train hard, eat healthily and stay focused I will have an Olympic gold medal at home one day.

My ambition is to win Olympic gold (nothing less!).

My first target is to be junior number one and to start picking up international medals.

In five years' time I would like to be British number one (comfortably) and have every chance of medalling at the 2016 Olympic Games.

There isn't much money in judo at the moment – you may as well be a student at university. Hopefully that will change by the time I'm at the top of the sport, but it's not about money anyway.

If I had to give up judo, I would like to be an architect.

Nathon, Robyn, Josh and Sam all have high hopes for the future. We wish them well.

Glossary

aerobic exercise Exercise that improves the efficiency of the cardiovascular system (heart and lungs).

breakfall A way of falling safely by spreading your body weight as you fall.

bridging A move during a judo hold-down when the defender lifts his or her hips and back off the mat. This move brings the hold-down count to a stop.

cadet In judo, a judoka who has won medals and has gone on to be chosen for his or her national squad.

cardiovascular exercise Exercise designed to improve the system that carries blood to and from all parts of the body.

circuit training A type of training that uses a series of different exercises repeated in a sequence.

conditioning Exercise that improves general physical fitness.

core strength The strength of the muscles in the trunk of the body.

cramp A sudden, sometimes painful, contraction of a muscle.

Dan The highest grade in judo.

dojo A judo training room.

drill An exercise that is practised over and over again to perfect a skill.

elite A group of people who are at the top level in their sport.

groundwork Any judo moves done on the floor.

hold-down A move in which a judoka holds his or her opponent down on the floor. A hold-down can win a judo contest if the opponent stays down for a specific length of time (between 15 and 25 seconds, depending on the level of competition).

judogi A judo uniform.

judoka Someone who takes part in judo.

jujitsu The ancient Japanese fighting art on which judo is based.

Kyu Senior judo grades.

lactic acid A substance produced in the muscles during exercise. Too much lactic acid can cause cramping pains.

martial art A fighting sport.

Mon The 18 junior judo grades.

motivate To encourage.

nutrition Describes the process by which the human body takes in and uses food.

obi A coloured judo belt that is worn to show what level a judoka has achieved.

physio (physiotherapy) The treatment of injuries with exercise.

reaping A type of judo throw in which the judoka uses his or her feet and legs to sweep an opponent's legs from beneath them.

repechage The system used to decide the winner and runners-up in major judo competitions.

stamina The ability to exercise at a high level for long periods.

submit To admit defeat.

tatami A judo mat.

tournament A series of contests to decide a winner.

Find out more

Judo terms

Ippon A judo throw, hold-down or submission that scores 10 points in a judo competition. It wins a contest outright.

Ippon-seoi-nage A one-armed shoulder throw.

Juji Gatame One of the armlocks used in judo.

Kansetsu Waza An armlock that puts pressure on the arm joint.

Kesa Gatame A judo hold-down.

Kumi Kata The art of taking a firm grip of your opponent by gripping his or her jacket.

Kuzushi Breaking your opponent's balance.

Nage Komi Judo throwing practice.

Nage Waza Judo throwing technique.

Ne Waza Groundwork in judo.

Osaekomi Waza Hold-downs.

Osoto Gari A large outer reaping throw.

Ouchi Gari A large inner reaping throw.

Randori Sparring practice.

Rei wo suru The bow that judoka make to each other at the beginning and end of every competition and practice session.

Shime Waza A stranglehold that puts pressure on the neck.

Tachi Waza The standing position in judo.

Tai Otoshi A body drop throw.

Toketa When a hold-down is broken.

Uchikomi A series of drills in judo training designed to build automatic reactions.

Uchi Mata An inner thigh throw.

Ukemi The techniques of falling or being thrown without getting hurt.

Wazari A throw or hold-down that scores 7 points in a judo competition.

Wazari-aweseti-ippon Two Wazari scores from a player make *Wazari-aweseti-ippon* – a 10-point score.

Yuko A throw or hold-down that scores 5 points in a judo competition.

Websites

www.britishjudo.org.uk
The website for British Judo. It has a lot of information on all aspects of judo including how to find your nearest judo club at:
www.britishjudo.org.uk/thesport/findclub.php

www.judoinfo.com/animate.htm
Watch animation of judo throws.

www.ijf.org/
The website of the International Judo Federation. It has a useful calendar of International judo events.

www.twoj.org/contents/links.html
Run by the official magazine of the British judo association, this website contains links to useful websites worldwide.

Books

Know Your Sport: Judo (Franklin Watts, 2007)
A guide to judo, with step-by-step photographs and explanations of some of the techniques, as well as profiles and statistics giving information about some of the world's greatest judoka.

Note to parents and teachers: every effort has been made by the Publishers to ensure that these websites are suitable for children, that they are of the highest educational value, and that they contain no inappropriate or offensive material. However, because of the nature of the Internet, it is impossible to guarantee that the contents of these sites will not be altered. We strongly advise that Internet access is supervised by a responsible adult.

Index